GRAPHIC MODERN HISTORY
COLD WAR CONFLICTS
THE KOREAN
WAR

By Gary Jeffrey & Illustrated by Terry Riley

 Crabtree Publishing Company

www.crabtreebooks.com

Crabtree Publishing Company
www.crabtreebooks.com
1-800-387-7650

Publishing in Canada
616 Welland Ave.
St. Catharines, ON
L2M 5V6

Published in the United States
PMB 59051, 350 Fifth Ave.
59th Floor,
New York, NY

Published in **2014 by CRABTREE PUBLISHING COMPANY.**

Printed in Hong Kong/092013/BK20130703

Copyright © **2013 David West Children's Books**

Created and produced by:

David West Children's Books

Project development, design, and concept:

David West Children's Books

Author and designer: Gary Jeffrey

Illustrator: Terry Riley

Editors: Lynn Peppas,

Kathy Middleton

Proofreader: Kelly McNiven

Project coordinator:

Kathy Middleton

Production coordinator and

Prepress technician:

Ken Wright

Print coordinator:

Margaret Amy Salter

Photographs:

p4r, U.S. Navy photo; p5t, U.S.
Defense Department, p5m,
United States Air Force, p5b, p6,
US Navy; p6t, p44b, p45t,
NARA; p7b, Cpl. McDonald;
p46, Corporal Thomas Marotta

Library and Archives Canada Cataloguing in Publication

Jeffrey, Gary, author
    The Korean War / by Gary Jeffrey and illustrated by
Terry Riley.

(Graphic modern history : Cold War conflicts)
Includes index.
Issued in print and electronic formats.
ISBN 978-0-7787-1234-3 (bound).--ISBN 978-0-7787-1238-1
(pbk.).--ISBN 978-1-4271-9345-2 (pdf).--ISBN 978-1-4271-9341-4
(html)

    1. Korean War, 1950-1953--Juvenile literature. 2. Korean
War, 1950-1953--Comic books, strips, etc. 3. Graphic novels.
I. Riley, Terry, illustrator II. Title. III. Series: Jeffrey, Gary.
Graphic modern history. Cold War conflicts

DS918.J35 2013   j951.904'2   C2013-904130-3
                                            C2013-904131-1

Library of Congress Cataloging-in-Publication Data

Jeffrey, Gary, author.
 The Korean War / by Gary Jeffrey and illustrated by Terry
Riley.
     pages cm. -- (Graphic modern history : cold war conflicts)
 Includes index.
 ISBN 978-0-7787-1234-3 (reinforced library binding) -- ISBN
978-0-7787-1238-1 (pbk.) -- ISBN 978-1-4271-9345-2 (electronic
pdf) -- ISBN 978-1-4271-9341-4 (electronic html)
 1. Korean War, 1950-1953--Comic books, strips, etc. 2. Korean
War, 1950-1953--Juvenile literature. 3. Korean War, 1950-1953--
United States--Comic books, strips, etc. 4. Korean War, 1950-
1953--United States--Juvenile literature. 5. Graphic novels.
I. Riley, Terry, illustrator. II. Title.

 DS918.J44 2014
 951.904'2--dc23
                                          2013023908

CONTENTS

LIGHTNING STRIKE

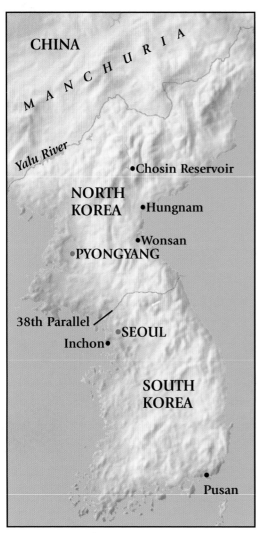

The Democratic People's Republic of Korea (DPRK) lies to the north of the 38th parallel. The Republic of Korea (ROK) lies to the south.

North Korean leader Kim Il-Sung had been schooled in the Soviet Union.

South Korean leader Dr. Syngman Rhee was a tyrannical "strongman."

In 1943, during World War II, Russia, Great Britain, and the United States agreed that when Korea was liberated from the Japanese, it would be run jointly until it could become independent.

CARVED UP

When Soviet forces invaded Japanese-held Manchuria in 1945, they advanced into northern Korea. Japan surrendered the rest of Korea to the Allies. Soviet leader Joseph Stalin agreed to divide control of Korea with the United States at the 38th parallel. This period marks the beginning of the Cold War between the United States and the Soviet Union. Although the two countries did not engage in battle directly, they competed instead for control or influence over other countries.

The United States had emerged from the war as the leading world superpower. Stalin wanted North Korea to be a communist buffer zone against American influence.

Meanwhile each of the new leaders in both North and South Korea considered themselves to be the rightful ruler of all of Korea. The North attempted to overthrow the South by funding insurgents. The communist uprising was brutally put down by South Korea.

INVASION

Kim Il-Sung sought to unite the two Koreas using military action. The People's Republic of China (PRC) and the Soviet Union agreed to support an invasion. In June of 1950, Kim Il-Sung's forces entered the demilitarized zone (DMZ), or the unoccupied land between the countries, promising to conquer South Korea in weeks.

Refugees move deeper into South Korea ahead of the rapidly advancing North Korean People's Army (NKPA).

LAST STAND AT PUSAN

With communist uprisings underway in Malaya and French Indochina, the United States saw the invasion as the start of a communist takeover of Southeast Asia. The United Nations agreed to send the United Nations Corps (UNC)— an international force, but mostly American— to aid a South Korean army that had already abandoned Seoul and was fleeing south ahead of the best Soviet armor and equipment.

U.S. infantrymen during the battle for Pusan

Mustangs flew vital ground attack missions to keep the North Koreans out.

Delaying actions were fought while UNC and South Korean forces put a defensive line together along the Naktong River in front of Pusan. American tanks arrived in time to fight Soviet T-34 tanks. UNC carried out air strikes around the clock. By mid September, North Korea's invasion force had been stopped.

5

COUNTER PUNCH

While the exhausted North Koreans pressed on at Pusan, U.S. Commander General Douglas MacArthur enacted his master-stroke—a large-scale amphibious invasion of Inchon.

War hero MacArthur had accepted the Japanese surrender in the Pacific.

STRATEGIC BRILLIANCE

MacArthur reasoned that by threatening the North Koreans from the rear and making a direct drive on Seoul, he could cut them off and relieve Pusan.

Landing at Inchon, however, was very risky. High and low tides were extreme, and the sea walls were tall. Luckily, Kim Il-Sung and his generals had left Inchon lightly defended, preferring to throw their troops into one last great assault at Pusan. Inchon was easily taken on September 15. Forty thousand marines landed. UNC forces held at the Second Battle of Naktong Bulge and successfully counter attacked. North Korea's invasion was in ruins.

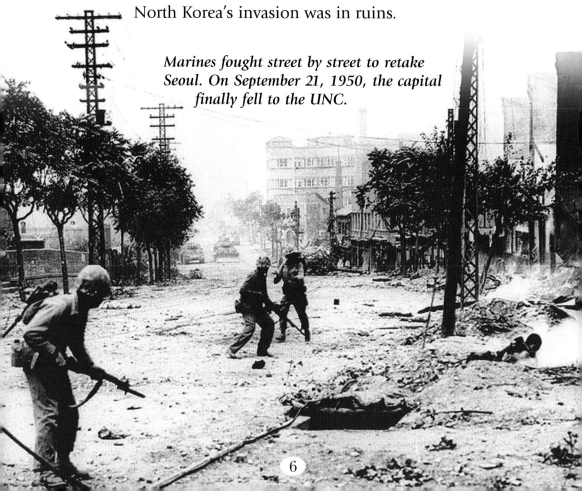

Marines fought street by street to retake Seoul. On September 21, 1950, the capital finally fell to the UNC.

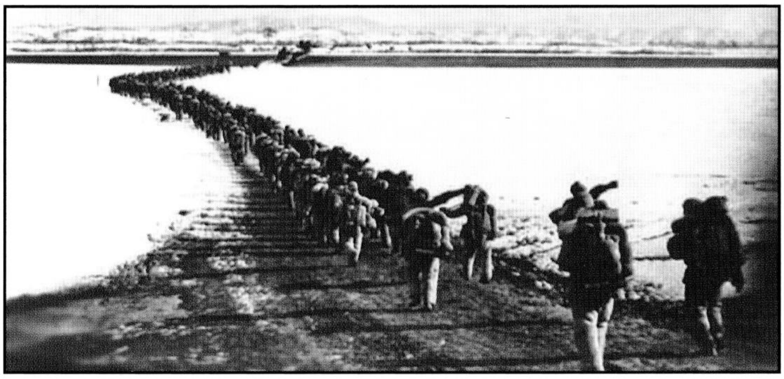

In 1950, from mid-October, a total of 300,000 Chinese soldiers, called the Chinese People's Volunteers (CPV), secretly crossed the frozen Yalu River into North Korea.

"Home by Christmas"

Spurred on by his overwhelming defeat of the North Koreans, MacArthur could not resist the idea of reuniting Korea under the UN banner. Landing reinforcements at Wonsan, he pushed toward the Chinese/Korean border with combined forces of 200,000 men.

Waves of Chinese Volunteers advanced toward the unprepared, stretched-out units of men who had expected to be home soon, not subjected to shock tactics such as infiltration and human wave attacks.

Lacking radios, CPV commanders signaled with bugles, drums, and whistles, disorienting UNC soldiers in the frozen night. Defeat came closest at Chosin Reservoir in the northeast as 120,000 Chinese infantry fought ferociously to try to encircle 103,000 X Corps marines.

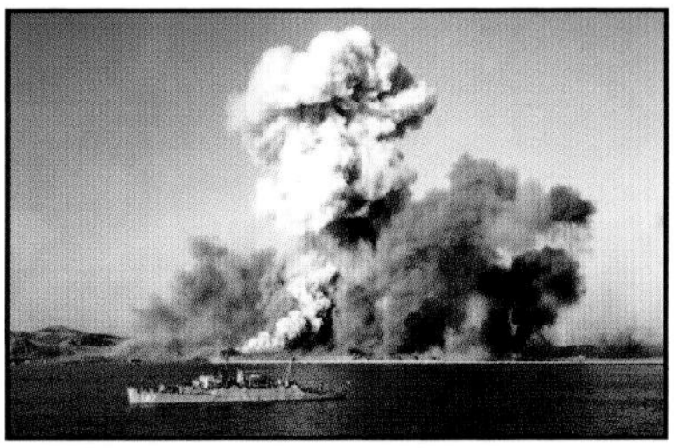

The Port of Hungnam was destroyed after the last marines were evacuated from northeast Korea.

X Corps marines watched as support aircraft dropped napalm on Chinese positions during the breakout at the Chosin Reservoir.

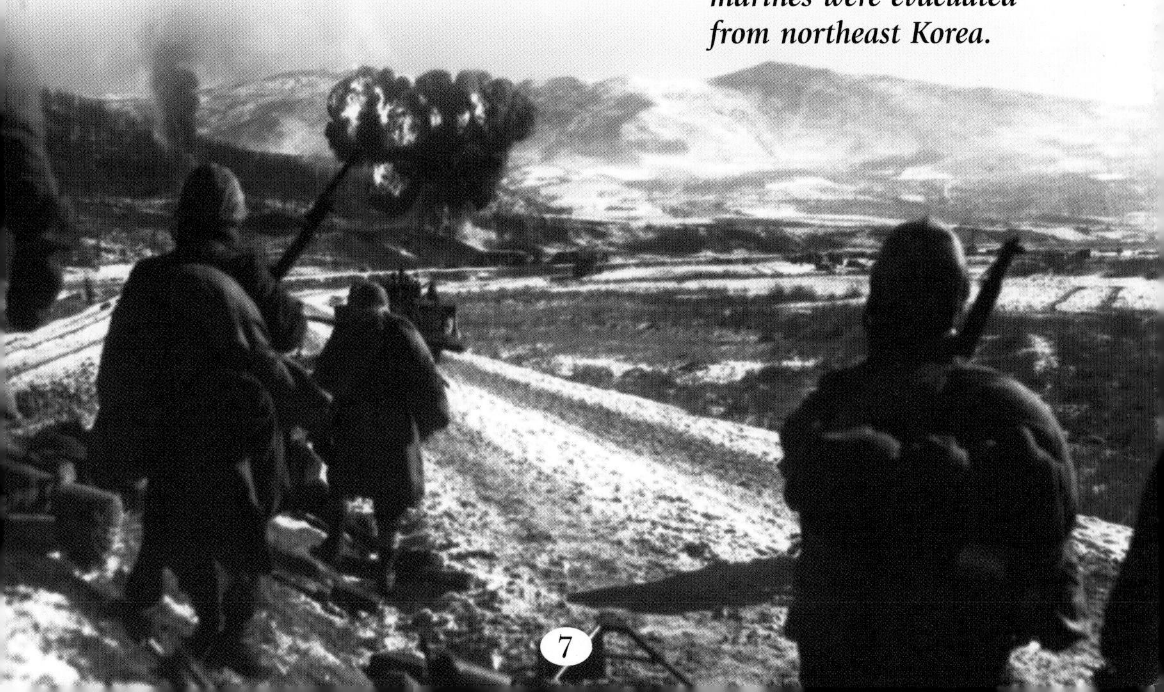

HELICOPTER RESCUE BEHIND ENEMY LINES

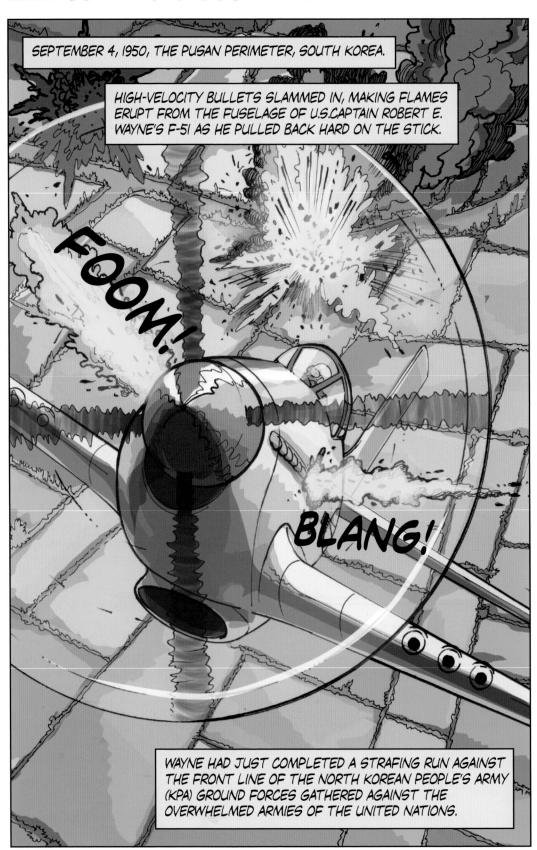

SEPTEMBER 4, 1950, THE PUSAN PERIMETER, SOUTH KOREA.

HIGH-VELOCITY BULLETS SLAMMED IN, MAKING FLAMES ERUPT FROM THE FUSELAGE OF U.S.CAPTAIN ROBERT E. WAYNE'S F-51 AS HE PULLED BACK HARD ON THE STICK.

FOOM!

BLANG!

WAYNE HAD JUST COMPLETED A STRAFING RUN AGAINST THE FRONT LINE OF THE NORTH KOREAN PEOPLE'S ARMY (KPA) GROUND FORCES GATHERED AGAINST THE OVERWHELMED ARMIES OF THE UNITED NATIONS.

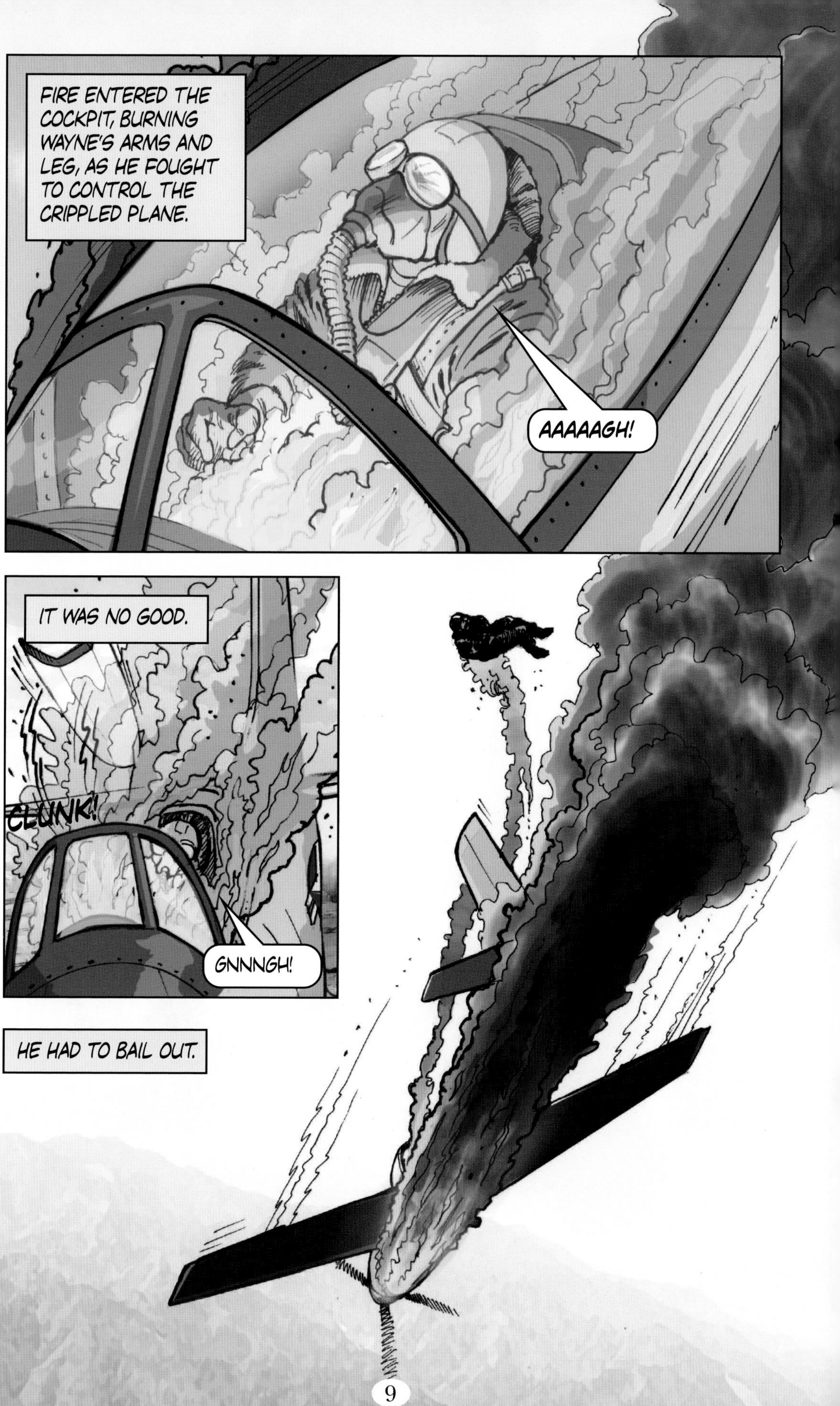
FIRE ENTERED THE COCKPIT, BURNING WAYNE'S ARMS AND LEG, AS HE FOUGHT TO CONTROL THE CRIPPLED PLANE.
AAAAAGH!
IT WAS NO GOOD.
CLUNK!
GNNNGH!
HE HAD TO BAIL OUT.

WAYNE DRIFTED DOWN TOWARD THE RICE PADDY FIELDS AS THE MUSTANG CRASHED TO EARTH.

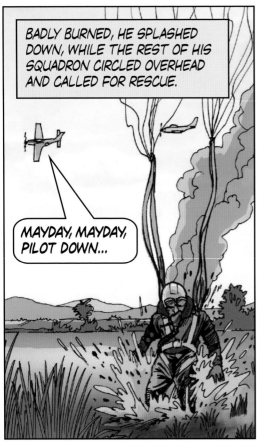

BADLY BURNED, HE SPLASHED DOWN, WHILE THE REST OF HIS SQUADRON CIRCLED OVERHEAD AND CALLED FOR RESCUE.

MAYDAY, MAYDAY, PILOT DOWN...

NEARBY UNITS OF THE ENEMY KPA HAD ALSO SPOTTED THE DOWNED AIRMAN.

THEY WOULD SHOW NO MERCY.

THREE HOURS LATER LIEUTENANT PAUL VAN BOVEN AND MEDIC JOHN FUENTES WERE SPEEDING TO THE PUSAN FRONT LINE IN AN H-5 MEDEVAC HELICOPTER.

THUCKA THUCKA

THE VOLUNTEER MISSION WAS RISKY. NORMALLY PILOTS BAILED OUT OVER THE OCEAN TO BE RESCUED BY FLOAT PLANES - NOT DOWN BEHIND ENEMY LINES.

I SEE THE WRECK!

THE H-5 WAS UNARMED AND UNARMORED.

OKAY, THERE'S SMOKE BUT...

11

OFF TO THEIR SIDE THEY SUDDENLY SPOTTED FOUR UNC F-51S MAKING A GROUND ATTACK RUN.

DRRRRRRRRRRR

THUNK

POW

ONE AFTER ANOTHER THE F-51S STRAFED THE EDGE OF THE PADDY.

IN THE NEXT FIELD, WAYNE STOOD UP, FRANTICALLY TORE OPEN HIS FLIGHT SUIT...

...AND WAVED HIS VEST.

OVER THERE!

VAN BOVEN MANEUVERED THE HELICOPTER TOWARD WAYNE, WATCHED BY A LONE KPA OFFICER WHO HAD SNEAKED OUT AHEAD.

THWACKA THWACKA

THE OFFICER DREW HIS PISTOL AND CHARGED.

SHA! SHA!*

THE MOVEMENT CAUGHT THE EYE OF F-51 PILOT CAPTAIN WHITE AS HE BANKED AROUND.

*DIE! DIE!

WHITE DIVED INTO THE ATTACK.

VRROOOM

SMALL ARMS FIRE HIT THE HELICOPTER'S FUSELAGE AS FUENTES SLID OPEN THE DOOR.

DING!

PRANG

THE KPA OFFICER HALTED AND AIMED HIS WEAPON AT THE RESCUERS.

THUCKA THUCKA

THE KPA OFFICER TURNED TOWARD THE SOUND OF THE BIG MUSTANG.

GOING TO HAVE TO BE A SHOT IN A MILLION...

VRRRAAAAAA

WHITE SLOWED THE AIRCRAFT AND PRESSED THE TRIGGER SWITCH.

ALL SIX MACHINE GUNS FIRED AT ONCE.

TAK! TAK! TAK!

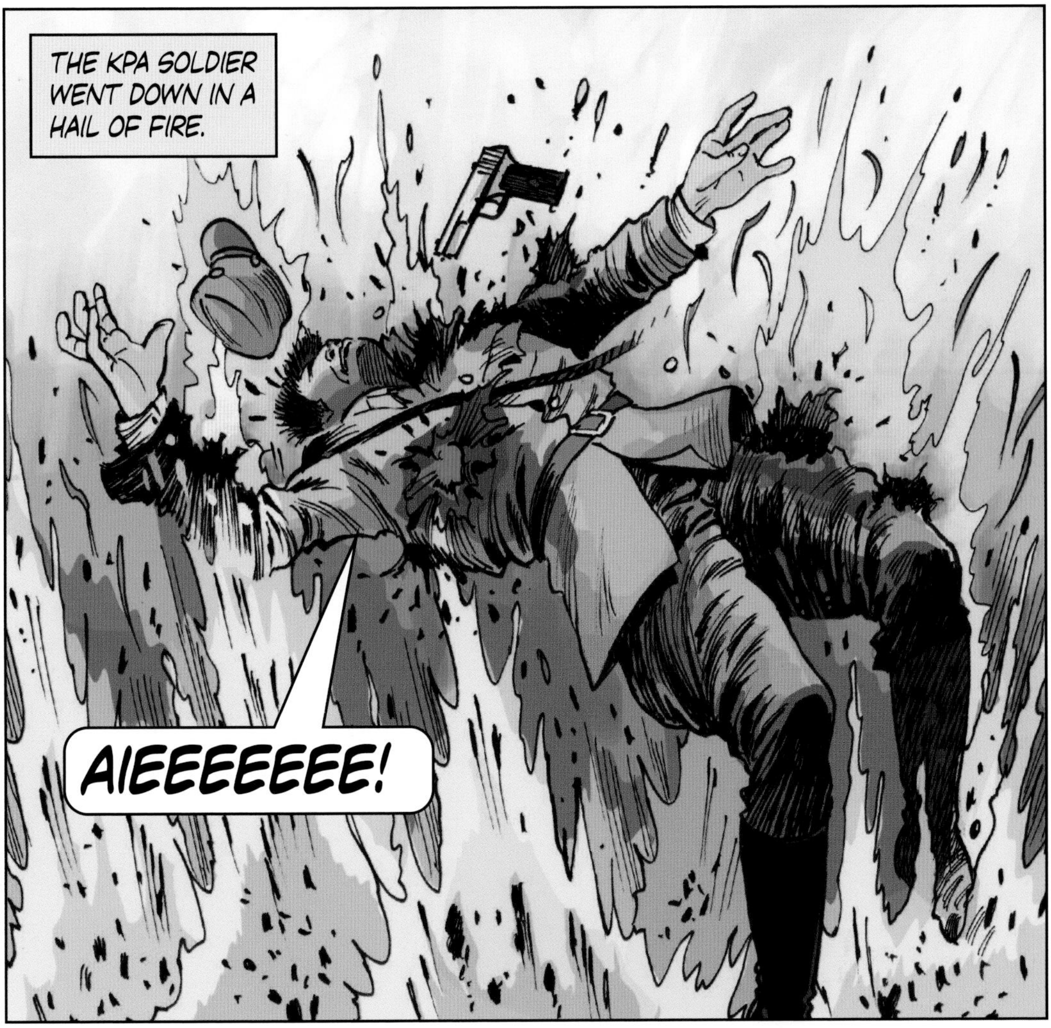
THE KPA SOLDIER WENT DOWN IN A HAIL OF FIRE.
AIEEEEEEE!

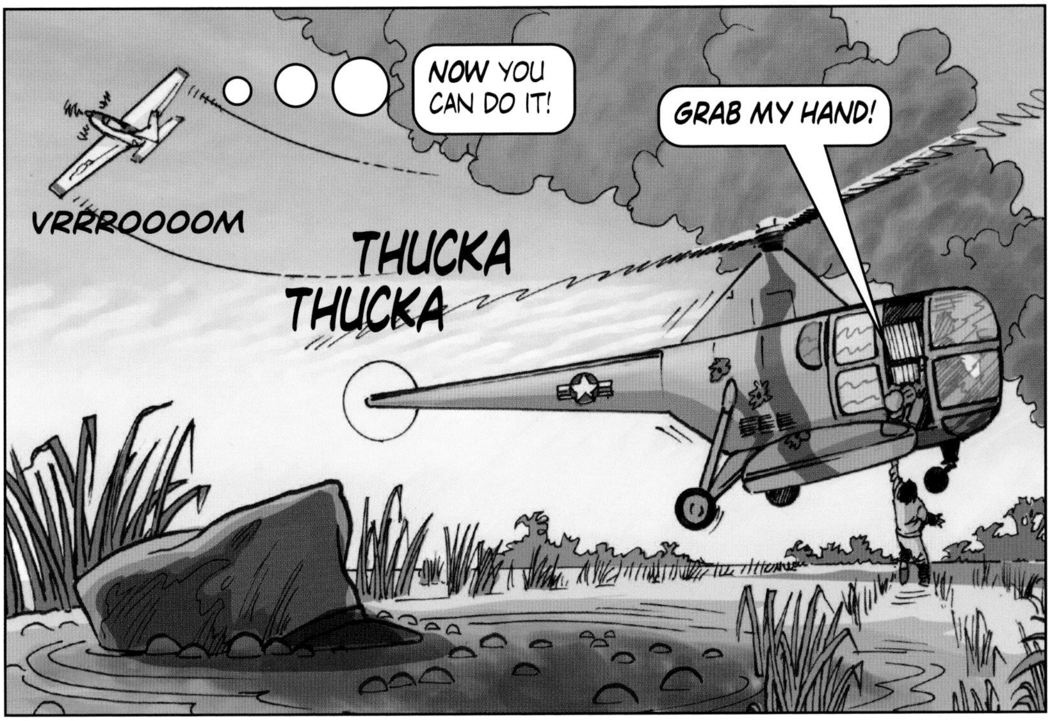
NOW YOU CAN DO IT!
GRAB MY HAND!
VRRROOOOM
THUCKA THUCKA

ONLY TWO F-51S REMAINED OVERHEAD AS ENEMY TRACER FIRE STREAKED ACROSS THE PADDY TOWARD THEM.

GOTCHA!

VAN BOVEN PULLED BACK ON THE PITCH CONTROL, SURGING THE H-5 FORWARD...

...THEN ALOFT, IN THE FIRST HELICOPTER RESCUE MISSION BEHIND ENEMY LINES OF THE KOREAN WAR.

THWACKA THWACKA

BASE, WE HAVE PILOT WAYNE AND ARE HEADING FOR HOME, OVER.

THE END

THE RELIEF OF FOX COMPANY: BATTLE OF CHOSIN RESERVOIR

DECEMBER 2, 1950, SOUTHWEST OF CHOSIN RESERVOIR, NORTH KOREA.

COME ON, PEARL, WE'RE GOING FOR A LITTLE STROLL.

A STAR SHELL LIT THE WAY AS 500 MARINES SET OUT CROSS-COUNTRY ON A NIGHT MISSION TO THE HILLS ABOVE TOKTONG PASS.

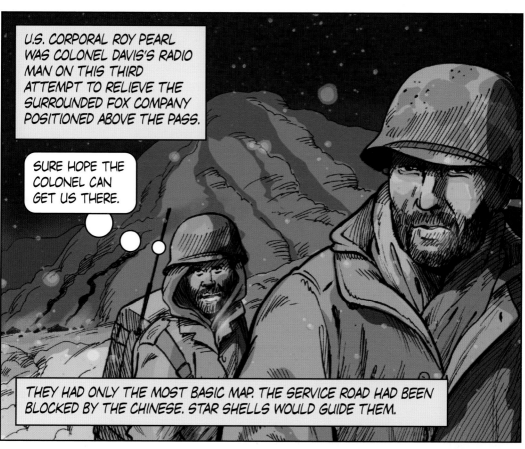

U.S. CORPORAL ROY PEARL WAS COLONEL DAVIS'S RADIO MAN ON THIS THIRD ATTEMPT TO RELIEVE THE SURROUNDED FOX COMPANY POSITIONED ABOVE THE PASS.

SURE HOPE THE COLONEL CAN GET US THERE.

THEY HAD ONLY THE MOST BASIC MAP. THE SERVICE ROAD HAD BEEN BLOCKED BY THE CHINESE. STAR SHELLS WOULD GUIDE THEM.

FAR AHEAD, U.S. LIEUTENANT "KURT" CHEW-EEN LEE LED 2ND RIFLES, BAKER COMPANY AT POINT, BREAKING A PATH THROUGH THE DENSELY PACKED SNOW.

TOKTONG PASS HAD TO BE HELD FOR X CORPS TO HAVE ANY CHANCE OF A BREAKOUT AT CHOSIN RESERVOIR.

THE TEMPERATURE PLUNGED, GLAZING THE FRESHLY BROKEN PATH WITH ICE. MEN, HEAVY WITH EXTRA AMMUNITION, STUMBLED AND FELL OUT OF LINE.

THE MARINES HAD ENDURED NEARLY CONSTANT FIGHTING SINCE THE CHINESE ATTACK AND WERE BONE-TIRED.

LEE HIMSELF WAS NURSING AN INJURED ELBOW, SHATTERED BY A SNIPER'S BULLET AT SUDONG GORGE FOUR WEEKS EARLIER.

THACK!

AS THEY DESCENDED INTO A DARK VALLEY, LEE TURNED TO SECOND LIEUTENANT JOE OWEN.

I HAVEN'T SEEN A STAR SHELL IN TEN MINUTES. IF WE DON'T SLOW DOWN WE'LL END UP GOING IN CIRCLES - OR OFF A CLIFF!

DOWN THE LINE AN AGITATED COLONEL DAVIS CHARGED PAST THE COLUMN AS PEARL TRIED TO KEEP UP.

CRUNCH! CRUNCH!

THE COLUMN'S DRIFTING TOO FAR SOUTH. GOING TO RUN INTO THE CHINESE ON THE ROAD BEFORE TOO LONG.

EVEN THOUGH THE MEN WERE BUNDLED UP, THEY COULD HEAR DAVIS CRASHING THROUGH THE SNOW.

QUIET! KNOCK OFF THE NOISE, BUDDY!

CRUNCH CRUNCH!

THAT'S THE BATTALION COMMANDER YOU'RE TALKING TO!

DAVIS FINALLY REACHED LEE AND GAVE HIM HIS INSTRUCTIONS.

THAT BRIGHT STAR THERE - HEAD US TOWARD THAT.

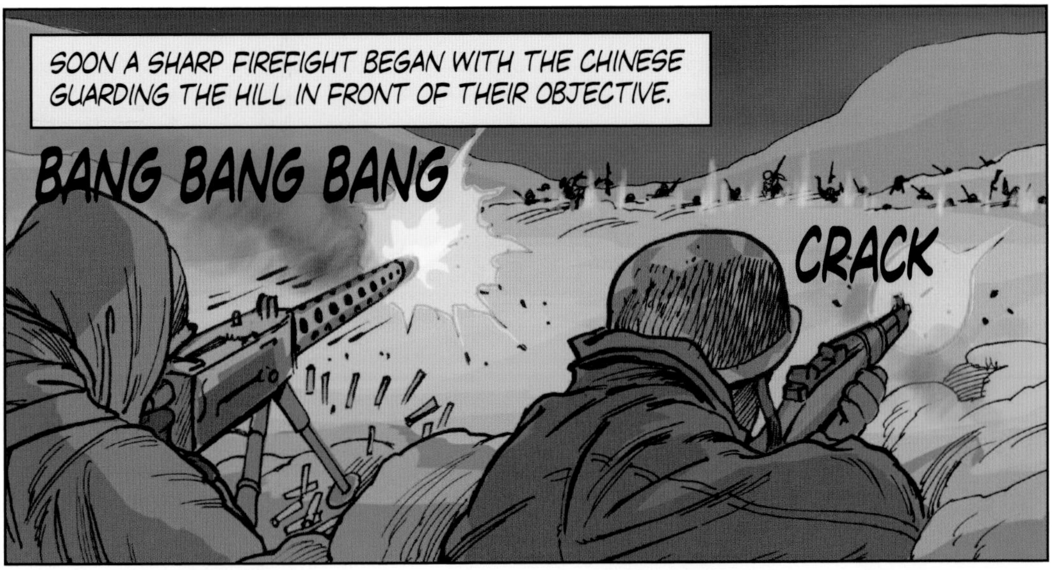
SOON A SHARP FIREFIGHT BEGAN WITH THE CHINESE GUARDING THE HILL IN FRONT OF THEIR OBJECTIVE.
BANG BANG BANG
CRACK

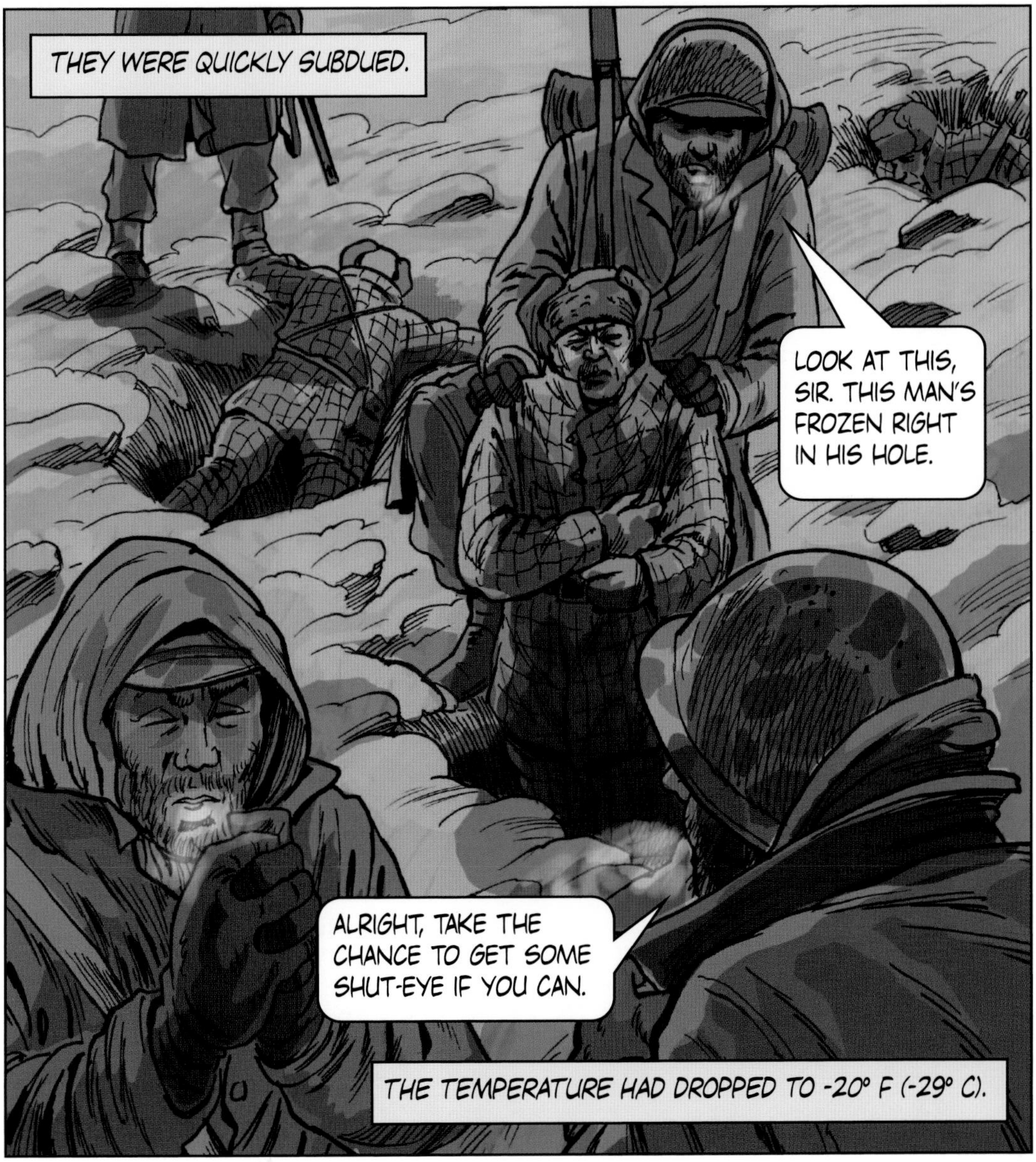
THEY WERE QUICKLY SUBDUED.
LOOK AT THIS, SIR. THIS MAN'S FROZEN RIGHT IN HIS HOLE.
ALRIGHT, TAKE THE CHANCE TO GET SOME SHUT-EYE IF YOU CAN.
THE TEMPERATURE HAD DROPPED TO -20° F (-29° C).

AT FIRST LIGHT THEY ASSAULTED HILL 1653 BUT WERE SOON PINNED DOWN.

THE CHINESE ARE DUG IN AT THOSE BOULDERS, SIR!

THEY'RE NOT GOING TO HOLD US UP!

DRRRRRRRRRR

LEE ORDERED HIS MEN TO FAN OUT.

ALL MEN TO OPEN FIRE ON MY COMMAND. WE'RE GOING TO **WALK IT.**

LED BY THEIR ONLY WORKING MACHINE GUN, THE MEN INITIATED "MARCHING FIRE," ADVANCING STEADILY UP THE HILLSIDE PRECEDED BY A HAIL OF BULLETS.

KLACK-KLACK-KLACK-

RRRRRRRRRR

CRACK-CRACK

LEE TOOK OUT TWO CPV* INFANTRYMEN WITH HIS SIDEARM AS HIS MEN MADE A BAYONET CHARGE.

RAAAAAA!

CRACK

*CHINESE PEOPLE'S VOLUNTEER ARMY

27

WHEN HE REACHED THE TOP, LEE WAS ASTONISHED TO SEE...

FOXHOLES ALL THE WAY DOWN TOWARD THE ROAD. THEY WERE EXPECTING AN ATTACK FROM THE OTHER DIRECTION!

IN FRONT OF HIM HE COULD SEE A LINE OF 20 CPV SOLDIERS FLEEING THROUGH THE SNOW.

VICTORY IS OURS.

AT LAST FOX COMPANY WAS RELIEVED. THE NUMBER OF DEAD PILED IN FRONT OF THE OUTPOST ASTONISHED THE RESCUERS.

THAT MUST HAVE BEEN SOME FIGHT.

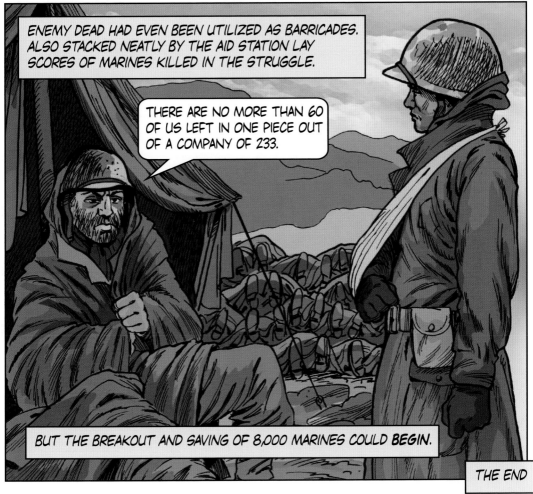

ENEMY DEAD HAD EVEN BEEN UTILIZED AS BARRICADES. ALSO STACKED NEATLY BY THE AID STATION LAY SCORES OF MARINES KILLED IN THE STRUGGLE.

THERE ARE NO MORE THAN 60 OF US LEFT IN ONE PIECE OUT OF A COMPANY OF 233.

BUT THE BREAKOUT AND SAVING OF 8,000 MARINES COULD BEGIN.

THE END

DUELING ON THE DECK
IN THE BATTLE OF "MIG ALLEY"

SEPTEMBER 15, 1952, OVER THE YALU RIVER, NORTHWEST KOREA.

USAF* CAPTAIN ROBINSON RISNER (CALL SIGN "JOHN RED LEAD") LINED UP THE MIG SQUARELY INSIDE HIS TARGET AIMING POINT.

HE WAS LEADING A GROUP OF FOUR F-86 SABRES ON A BOMBER ESCORT MISSION WHEN THE ENEMY MIG-15S POPPED UP FROM A BASE OVER THE CHINESE BORDER.

*USAF - UNITED STATES AIR FORCE

EVEN THOUGH HE WAS AT MAXIMUM RANGE, HIS RADAR RANGING GUNSIGHT WOULD COMPENSATE FOR THE BULLET'S CURVING PATH.

HE PRESSED THE TRIGGER AND RELEASED A VOLLEY OF FIFTY CALIBER* BULLETS.

TIKKA
TIKKA
TIKKA

THE COCKPIT OF THE FOURTH MIG IN LINE EXPLODED INTO FRAGMENTS.

BOOM!

*12.95 MILLIMETER

31

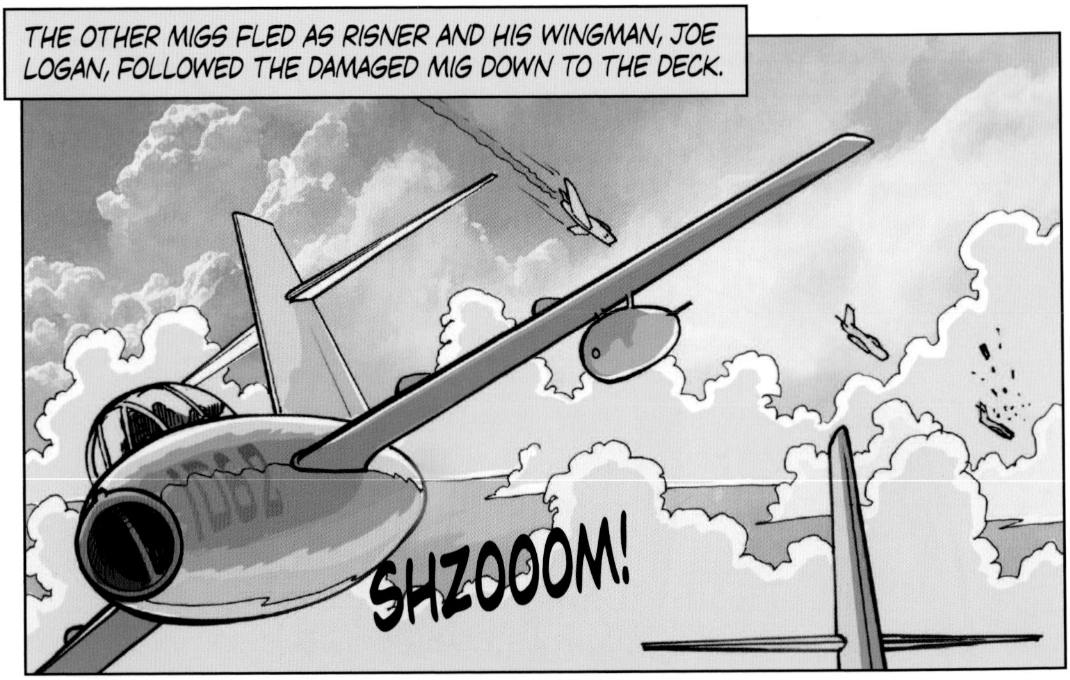
THE OTHER MIGS FLED AS RISNER AND HIS WINGMAN, JOE LOGAN, FOLLOWED THE DAMAGED MIG DOWN TO THE DECK.
SHZOOOM!

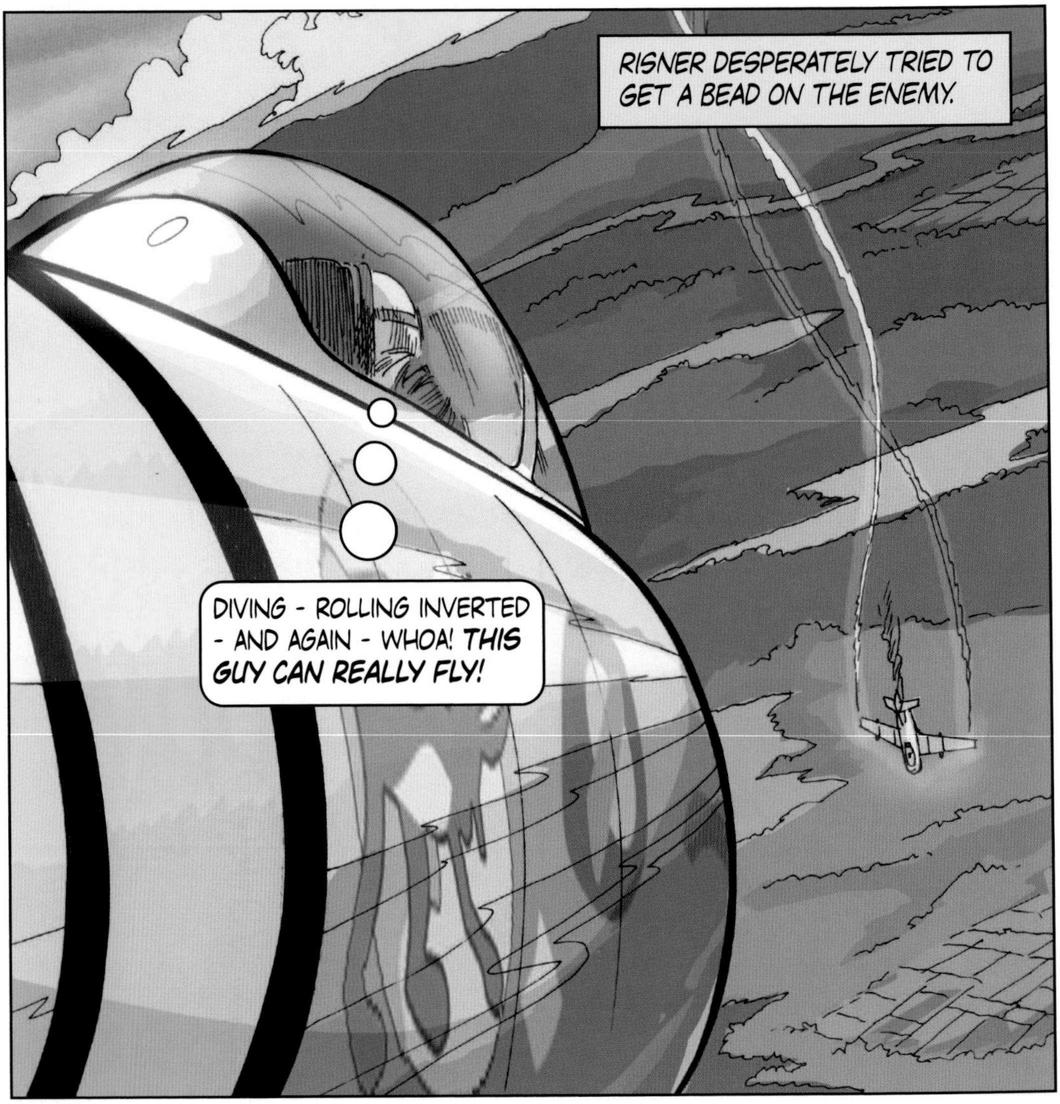
RISNER DESPERATELY TRIED TO GET A BEAD ON THE ENEMY.
DIVING - ROLLING INVERTED - AND AGAIN - WHOA! THIS GUY CAN REALLY FLY!

THE FLYER WAS ONE OF THE VETERAN SOVIET PILOTS NICKNAMED "HONCHOS" BY THE USAF.

AS HIS CRAFT ROCKETED EARTHWARD UPSIDE DOWN, HE PULLED BACK HARD ON THE STICK.

AN INVERTED LOOP WOULD ENABLE HIM TO CHANGE DIRECTION FAST.

HE'S GOING FOR A SPLIT-S?!

SCREEEEEEE

RISNER WAITED FOR THE TELL-TALE FIREBALL ON THE GROUND.

NO WAY IS HE GOING TO MAKE THAT...

THIS IS GOING TO BE THE EASIEST KILL I'VE EVER HAD!

BY THE TIGHTEST POSSIBLE MARGIN, THE MIG CLEARED THE GROUND, SENDING ROCKS SKITTERING ACROSS THE DRY RIVERBED.

BLAST!

HE MADE IT!

RISNER PUSHED THE THROTTLE AND TOOK OFF IN PURSUIT.

CLUNK!

BLASTED BY THE MIG'S JET TRAIL, ROCKS BOUNCED INTO THE F-86'S FUSELAGE.

OH, BOY!

THUNK

CLANK!

THE HONCHO SUDDENLY HIT HIS AIR BRAKES TO CHOP SPEED AND TRY TO MAKE RISNER OVERSHOOT.

DWEEEEE

RISNER ROLLED OVER THE TOP TO BLEED OFF AIRSPEED AND STAY ON THE MIG'S SIX O'CLOCK*.

*RIGHT BEHIND HIM

THE HONCHO FIREWALLED THE THROTTLE...

CLUNK

...PULLING MAXIMUM GS.

RISNER LET OFF A FEW SHOTS.

BADDA
BADDA
BADDA

THERE YOU GO!

BULLETS THUDDED INTO THE MIG'S TAIL, CAUSING DEBRIS TO BREAK AWAY.

PLOOM!

THE MIG FLIPPED INVERTED AND BLASTED ALONG THE CURVE OF A LOW HILL AS THEY DESCENDED TO THE RIVERBED AGAIN.

ROOAAAR!

NO WAY AM I TRYING THAT!

THE HONCHO DECELERATED RAPIDLY ONCE MORE.

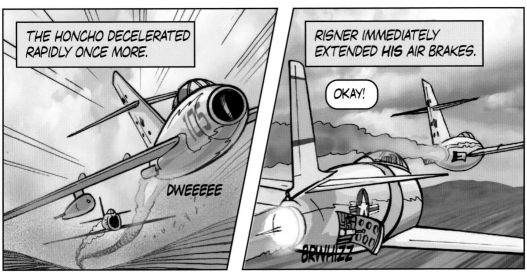

DWEEEEE

RISNER IMMEDIATELY EXTENDED **HIS** AIR BRAKES.

OKAY!

BRWHIZZ

THE TWO AIRCRAFT DREW LEVEL. RISNER TURNED TO LOOK AT HIS ADVERSARY...

...WHO SHOOK HIS FIST.

UNBELIEVABLE!

THE MIG SUDDENLY SCREAMED ACROSS HIS PATH AS FLAK BLOSSOMED IN THE AIR.

WHAT THE....!?

THEY HAD REACHED THE MIG'S HOME FIELD.

TOO LOW TO GET A SHOT!

THE HONCHO WANTED TO LAND. HE MADE A CLIMBING TURN TO COME AROUND AGAIN.

THAT'S IT!

RISNER LINED UP HIS PIPPER*...

I'VE GOT YOU **HEAVY**!

*GUNFIRE DIRECTOR

...AND BLASTED HIS GUNS.

DRRRRRRR

INCENDIARIES LIT UP THE MIG'S STARBOARD WING, SETTING IT ON FIRE.

KROOM

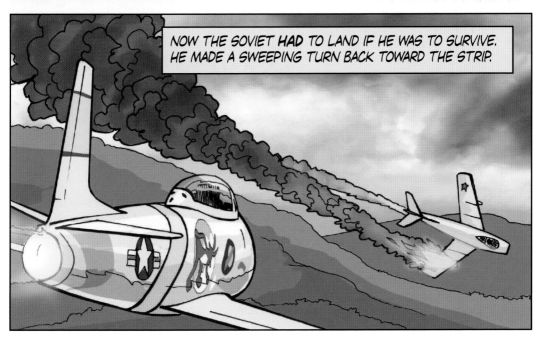

NOW THE SOVIET **HAD** TO LAND IF HE WAS TO SURVIVE. HE MADE A SWEEPING TURN BACK TOWARD THE STRIP.

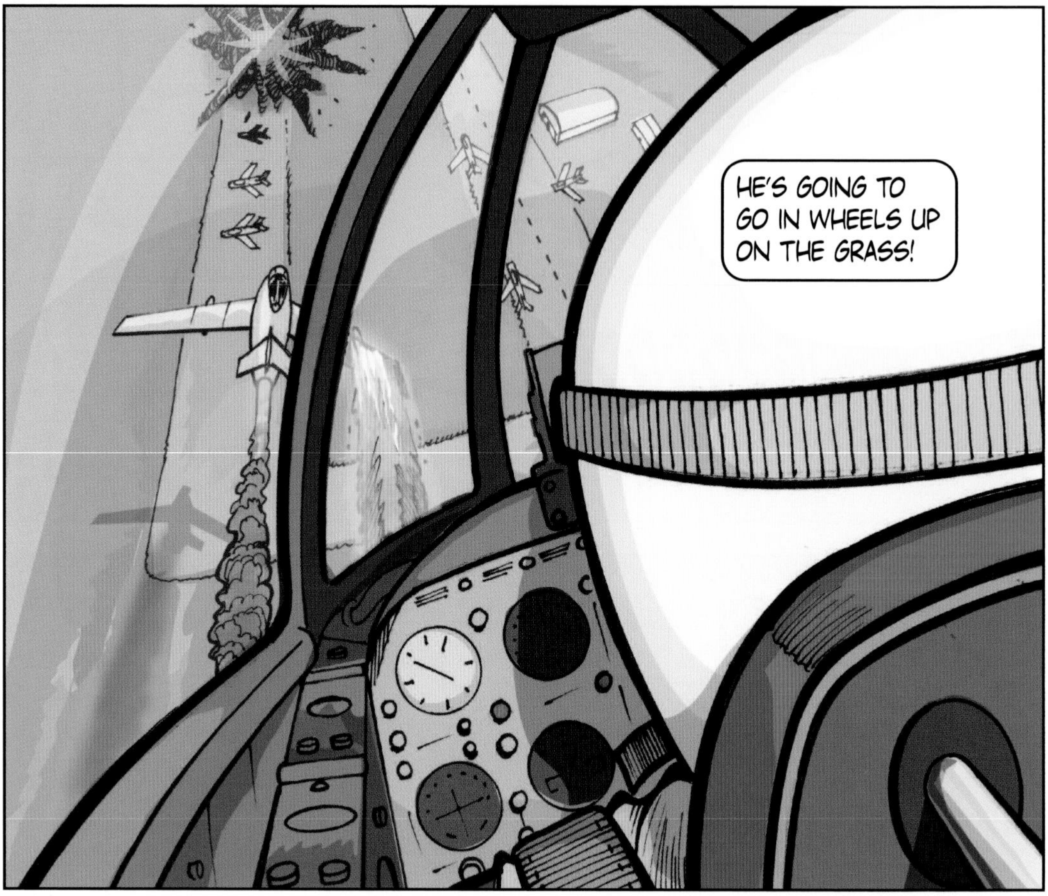
HE'S GOING TO GO IN WHEELS UP ON THE GRASS!

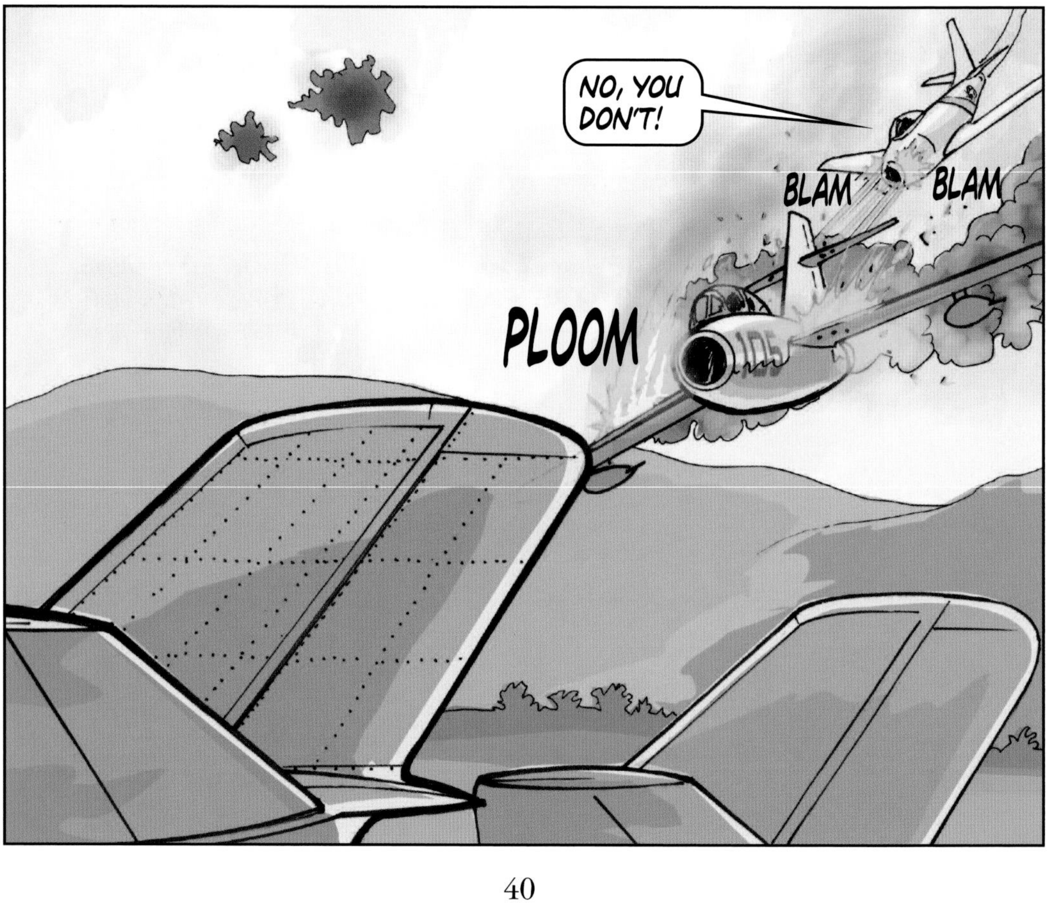
NO, YOU DON'T!
BLAM
BLAM
PLOOM
105

THE MIG SMASHED TO EARTH SENDING BLAZING DEBRIS THROUGH A WHOLE ROW OF PARKED FIGHTERS.

LEAD, I THINK YOU JUST BLEW UP THEIR ENTIRE AIR FORCE!

BOOOOM

TIME TO GET OUT OF DODGE.

AS THEY LEFT AN ANTI-AIRCRAFT SHELL EXPLODED UNDER LOGAN'S PLANE.

KRAK

ON THE RETURN FLIGHT...

LEAD, I SEEM TO BE LOSING FUEL, COULD YOU CHECK ME OUT?

RISNER MANEUVERED UNDERNEATH.

BOY, IT'S POURING OUT. HE'S NOT GOING TO MAKE IT.

BAILING OUT OVER CHINA WAS UNTHINKABLE. THEY WEREN'T "OFFICIALLY" ALLOWED TO CROSS THE BORDER.

JOE, I'M GOING TO TRY SOMETHING. I'LL NEED YOU TO SHUT YOUR ENGINE DOWN.

RISNER CAREFULLY MANEUVERED HIS SABRE'S NOSE INTO LOGAN'S TAILPIPE.

OKAY - SHUT OFF.

HYDRAULIC FLUID AND FUEL FOULED RISNER'S CANOPY...

...AS HE PUSHED THE CRIPPLED F-86 ON.

ROOAAR

JUST HAVE TO REACH CHO-DO ISLAND...

OVER THE OCEAN, JOE LOGAN FINALLY BAILED OUT.

"ROBBY, I'LL SEE YOU AT THE BASE TONIGHT."

"A-OKAY!"

CLUNK!

TRAGICALLY, AT SPLASHDOWN, LOGAN GOT CAUGHT IN HIS PARACHUTE LINES AND DROWNED.

THE HONCHO WAS RISNER'S SECOND KILL. HE WENT ON TO SCORE SIX MORE, MAKING HIM A KOREAN WAR ACE.

THE END

DEADLOCK

The Chinese onslaught forced all UNC armies back behind the 38th parallel—the longest retreat in U.S. Army history. The panicked UNC command considered quitting the peninsula altogether.

The U.S. Army used howitzers in the fighting north of the 38th parallel.

SLUGGING MATCH

The news reached Chinese leader Mao Zedong who ordered his army to cross the DMZ and take Seoul. The invasion reenergized the defenders. MacArthur was calling for direct action against the Chinese mainland—even the use of the atomic bomb. U.S. President Truman could see that attempting total victory over China and North Korea was unrealistic. The UNC opted instead to fight a "limited war" of simply preserving South Korea.

They called for a ceasefire—which the Chinese rejected. The Chinese wanted all UNC forces out of South Korea. The UNC, now under the command of U.S. General Matthew Ridgway, needed to win back ground from the Chinese to force them to the negotiating table. The Chinese and North Koreans were determined to land a killer blow.

The intensity and tactics of the war meant that casualties were high. The UNC benefited from having helicopters to evacuate the wounded to mobile medical (MASH) stations close to the front line.

AIR SUPREMACY

While the infantry war moved back and forth across the 38th parallel, UNC bomber aircraft attacked the communist supply lines that stretched across North Korea.

Lined up against them were hundreds of Soviet-built MiG jet Interceptors. North American F-86s and MiG-15s fought dogfights south of the Yalu River in an area that became known as "MiG Alley." The outnumbered U.S. pilots–many veterans of World War II–evened the odds with their great flying skill.

A USAF F-80 drops a napalm canister on a North Korean industrial target. Power plants and cities were also targeted to weaken the North's morale.

Chinese troops demonstrated their never-say-die spirit by throwing rocks at advancing UNC soldiers when their ammo ran out.

BITTER TO THE END

The unexpected death of Soviet leader Joseph Stalin in March of 1953 weakened the communists' resolve to continue the war.

The war ended four months later. The UNC suffered more than 178,000 killed (including 33,686 American combat deaths) and half a million wounded. The Chinese and North Koreans had up to 1.4 million killed and wounded. Civilian casualties reached 2.5 million. Today, Korea remains divided at the armistice line.

GLOSSARY

armistice A temporary halt in the conflict between two warring groups

breakout A military operation to free surrounded forces

buffer zone An area of land between two countries in conflict with each other that protects either country from immediate attack

call sign A combination of letters or words used to identify different military facilities, units, or personnel

canopy A transparent, weatherproof cover over an aircraft's cockpit

Cold War A period of political tension from 1947 to 1990 during which communist countries led by the Soviet Union and democratic countries from the West led by the United States competed militarily. Each side tried to control or influence unstable countries around the world in an effort to spread their own styles of government.

column A long line of troops

decelerated Reduced speed

deck The ground

dogfights Close combat between fighter aircraft

flak Anti-aircraft fire

fuselage The main body of an aircraft, holding cargo or people

Gs Units of force that gravity puts on a pilot's body during acceleration

human wave attacks A plan of attack in which heavily concentrated formations of soldiers move forward against an enemy, intending to overrun them and engage in hand-to-hand combat

GIs on a M26 tank await an enemy advance near the Naktong River, in 1950.

ideologies Sets of beliefs that form the basis of political or economic systems

incendiaries (ammunition) Ammunition that ignites when fired to cause the target to catch fire

infiltration The process of passing into an enemy position

inverted loop When a plane executes a circular loop but instead of facing inward the pilot faces outward

jet trail A long, thin cloud of condensation or vapor behind an aircraft

MASH Mobile Army Surgical Hospital

medevac Medical evacuation

MiG-15 One of the first successful swept-wing jet fighters developed by the Soviet Union

napalm An extremely sticky jellied gasoline mixture used in bombs that sticks to skin and anything else it touches and which causes severe burns when set on fire

perimeter A military boundary defining where enemy territory begins

pitch control The helicopter pilot's control lever that operates vertical movement known as the collective pitch control, or collective lever

point The first and most exposed position in a military combat formation, that is, the lead soldier or unit advancing through hostile territory

relieved To be replaced by another person or group after a duty is completed

sidearm A small weapon such as a pistol worn at the side or waist

star shell An artillery shell that explodes in midair with a shower of lights, used for illumination and signaling

strafing Attacking repeatedly with bombs or machine gun fire from low-flying aircraft

T-34 A Soviet medium tank produced from 1940 to 1958

throttle A lever that controls the thrust of an aircraft's engines

tracer fire Chemical trails from ammunition that help shooters correct their aim

United Nations An international organization made up of 192 states to stop wars between countries and achieve lasting world peace

veteran A person who has had long service or experience in the armed forces

wingman A pilot whose aircraft is positioned behind and outside the leading aircraft in a formation

INDEX